# *A Gift for Jesus*

*by*
Joan Summer

WINEPRESS WP PUBLISHING

Printed in Korea

Packaged by WinePress Publishing, PO Box 428, Enumclaw, WA 98022. The views expressed or implied in this work do not necessarily reflect those of WinePress Publishing. The author is ultimately responsible for the design, content, and editorial accuracy of this work.



ISBN 1-57921-421-5
Library of Congress Catalog Card Number: 2001096000

*To my husband Bob*
*with love.*

Long ago, on a starry night,
In a stable very small
A baby was born, called Jesus
God sent His Son to us all.

Wise men came to worship Him,
Oh, the wisest men they were,
For they brought Him the finest gifts
Of gold, frankincense, and myrrh.

I wonder, if *I* gave Him a gift,
What would be the best of all?
I'd have to sit and think and think. . . .
Should it be big or small?

Now, if I were a great wise king
And sat upon a throne
I think I'd give Him a jeweled crown
To be His very own.

Or, if I were a big, tall cowboy,
With my guns and cowboy hat;
I'd give Him my palomino pony,
What would He think of that?

If I were the captain of a ship,
Sailing the great blue sea,
I'd bring Him some shiny seashells
Just to remember me.

If I were a handsome pirate
With a bulging treasure chest,
I'd give Him all my treasure.
Would He like that the best?

If I were a big, brave soldier,
Fighting in my country's war,
I'd give Him all my medals
And wish I could give Him more.

If I were an Indian chief,
With tomahawk and tom-toms too
I'd give Him my headdress of feathers,
All red, and yellow, and blue.

If I were a hard-working farmer,
With my fields of corn and wheat;
I'd bring Him a lamb or a chicken,
And place it at His feet.

But I'm just me, and I don't have a lot—
Just some marbles, and some shiny rocks.
Maybe He'd like my rocking horse
Or my books, or my favorite blocks.

Now what could I give to Jesus?
Why, it's as simple as can be—
What will I give Jesus?
Of course—I'll give Him *me!*

To order additional copies of

*A Gift for Jesus*

Contact

WinePress Publishing
PO Box 428
Enumclaw, WA 98022

(877) 421-READ (7323)

www.winepresspub.com